The Vanity of Thoughts

PURITAN
Treasures for Today

SERIES EDITORS
Joel R. Beeke & Jay T. Collier

Interest in the Puritans continues to grow, but many people find the reading of these giants of the faith a bit unnerving. This series seeks to overcome that barrier by presenting Puritan books that are convenient in size and unintimidating in length. Each book is carefully edited with modern readers in mind, smoothing out difficult language of a bygone era while retaining the meaning of the original authors. Books for the series are thoughtfully selected to provide some of the best counsel on important subjects that people continue to wrestle with today.

The Vanity
of Thoughts

Thomas Goodwin

Edited by
Brian G. Hedges

RHB

Reformation Heritage Books
Grand Rapids, Michigan

The Vanity of Thoughts
© 2024 by Reformation Heritage Books

Reformation Heritage Books
3070 29th St. SE
Grand Rapids, MI 49512
616-977-0889
orders@heritagebooks.org
www.heritagebooks.org

Unless otherwise indicated, Scripture taken from the King James Version. In the public domain.

Scripture marked NKJV taken from the New King James Version®. Copyright © 1982 by Thomas Nelson. Used by permission. All rights reserved.

Printed in the United States of America
24 25 26 27 28 29/10 9 8 7 6 5 4 3 2 1

Library of Congress Cataloging-in-Publication Data

Names: Goodwin, Thomas, 1600-1680, author. | Hedges, Brian G., editor.
Title: The vanity of thoughts / Thomas Goodwin ; edited by Brian G. Hedges.
Description: Grand Rapids, Michigan : Reformation Heritage Books, [2024] |
    Series: Puritan treasures for today | Includes bibliographical references.
Identifiers: LCCN 2024033152 (print) | LCCN 2024033153 (ebook) |
    ISBN 9798886861426 (paperback) | ISBN 9798886861433 (epub)
Subjects: LCSH: Puritans—England—History. | Goodwin, Thomas, 1600-1680. |
    Pride and vanity—Religious aspects—Christianity. | Sin.
Classification: LCC BX9333 .G66 2024 (print) | LCC BX9333 (ebook) |
    DDC 241.3—dc23/eng/20240725
LC record available at https://lccn.loc.gov/2024033152
LC ebook record available at https://lccn.loc.gov/2024033153

Table of Contents

Preface

We live in the age of distraction. Screens dominate our daily lives. Images flash across our minds with the speed of lightning. This constant barrage of texts, tweets, memes, and GIFs has diminished our capacity for deep thought. As Nicolas Carr, in his book *The Shallows*, observed,

> What the Net seems to be doing is chipping away my capacity for concentration and contemplation. Whether I'm online or not, my mind now expects to take in information the way the Net distributes it: in a swiftly moving stream of particles. Once I was a scuba diver in the sea of words. Now I zip along the surface like a guy on a Jet Ski.[1]

Surrounded as we are by technologies of diversion and distraction, the biblical mandate to bring "into

---

1. Nicolas Carr, *The Shallows: What the Internet Is Doing to Our Brains: Updated Edition* (New York: W. W. Norton & Company, 2020), 6–7.

captivity every thought to the obedience of Christ"
(2 Cor. 10:5) is both more difficult and more necessary
than ever.

The Scriptures constantly remind us that God cares
about our inner world, the life of the mind:

> A good man out of the good treasure of the heart
> bringeth forth good things: and an evil man out
> of the evil treasure bringeth forth evil things.
> (Matt. 12:35)

> For the LORD seeth not as man seeth; for man
> looketh on the outward appearance, but the LORD
> looketh on the heart. (1 Sam. 16:7)

> For as he thinketh in his heart, so is he. (Prov. 23:7)

Our thought lives matter.

In contrast to the superficiality of our world, the sev-
enteenth-century English Puritans studied the depths of
Scripture and the human heart. One of the most eminent
divines from this era was Thomas Goodwin (1600–
1680), author of *The Vanity of Thoughts Discovered with
Their Danger and Cure.*

The Life of Thomas Goodwin

Goodwin was born "in Rollesby, near Yarmouth in Nor-
folk, an area known for Puritan resistance to government
persecution."[2] As a boy, he had a sensitive conscience, and

---

2. Joel Beeke and Randall J. Pederson, *Meet the Puritans: With*

"from the age of six, he had such vivid impressions of the Holy Spirit that he wept for his sin and had 'flashes of joy upon thoughts of the things of God.'"[3] But despite this early spiritual sensitivity, his conversion and settled assurance in Christ did not come until much later.

Goodwin was educated at Christ's College in Cambridge and as a teenager listened to the sermons of Richard Sibbes (1577–1635), "the Sweet Dropper." But this was short-lived, and Goodwin became enamored with another style of preaching that focused on flights of eloquence and flashy displays of scholarship. In his biographical sketch of Goodwin, James Reid (1750–1837) said:

> Mr. Goodwin was then ignorant in a great degree both of the corruption of his nature, and of the necessity and worth of Jesus Christ. He pursued vain wisdom, and leaned unto his own understanding. He walked in the vanity of his mind, seeking applause and preferment. But Almighty God, in the unsearchable riches of his grace, was pleased to change his heart, and to turn the course of his life to his own service and glory.[4]

---

a Guide to Modern Reprints (Grand Rapids: Reformation Heritage Books, 2007), 265.

3. Beeke and Pederson, *Meet the Puritans*, 265.

4. James Reid, *Memoirs of the Westminster Divines* (1811; repr., Edinburgh: Banner of Truth, 1982), 1:320.

This change began when Goodwin was twenty years old, after attending a funeral where he heard Thomas Bainbridge (bap. 1574, d. 1646) preach on repentance. Deeply convicted of his sins, Goodwin began to amend his life and aligned himself with the theological tradition of Puritans such as William Perkins (1558–1602), Richard Sibbes, and John Preston (1587–1628).[5] But he would still spend the next seven years searching for personal assurance of his good standing in Christ. Goodwin later wrote of this spiritual struggle:

> I was diverted from Christ for several years, to search only into the signs of grace in me. It was almost seven years ere I was taken off to live by faith on Christ, and God's free love, which are alike the object of faith.[6]

In 1628, Goodwin was appointed lecturer of Trinity Church in Cambridge. Four years later, he became vicar. But, under the influence of John Cotton (1585–1652), Goodwin began to adopt the principles of Nonconformity, left the Church of England, and became an Independent. In 1638, he married Elizabeth Prescott. Soon after, they sought refuge in the Netherlands "because of increasing restrictions against preaching with threats of fines and imprisonment."[7]

---

5. Beeke and Pederson, *Meet the Puritans*, 268.

6. Beeke and Pederson, *Meet the Puritans*, 268.

7. Beeke and Pederson, *Meet the Puritans*, 269.

In the 1640s, Goodwin returned to England and eventually became a member of the Westminster Assembly, where he was a stalwart representative of Independency. "Records of the 243 sessions of the assembly indicate that Goodwin gave more addresses than any other divine—357 in all."[8] Along with William Bridge (ca. 1600–1670), Philip Nye (ca. 1595–1672), Jeremiah Burroughs (1599–1646), and Sidrach Simpson (ca. 1600–1655), Goodwin was one of the "Five Dissenting Brethren" who presented their views to the Assembly in *An Apologeticall Narration*, published in 1644.

Elizabeth died in the 1640s, leaving Goodwin with a daughter. Then in 1649, he wed Mary Hammond. He and Mary had four children, two of which died in infancy. In 1650, Goodwin became president of Magdalen College in Oxford and was a chaplain and advisor to Oliver Cromwell during the Interregnum period. He also helped start an Independent church, where he preached alongside Stephen Charnock (1628–1680), another Puritan known today for his magnificent book *The Existence and Attributes of God*.

In 1658, Goodwin was instrumental in drawing up the Savoy Declaration of Faith and Order, a confession of faith modeled on the Westminster Confession of Faith and adopted by 120 congregations. Following the restoration of the monarchy and the accession of Charles II

---

8. Beeke and Pederson, *Meet the Puritans*, 270.

in 1660, Goodwin left Oxford but continued to preach throughout the period of persecution following the 1662 Act of Uniformity.

In his later years, Goodwin "spent much of his time in religious retirement, in prayer, reading and meditation.... Though he read much, he spent more time in thinking, and it was by intense thought that he made himself master of the subject of his discourse."[9] During the illness that preceded his death, Goodwin said, "I am going to the Three Persons, with whom I have had communion. They have taken me, I did not take them. I shall be changed in the twinkling of an eye. All my lusts and corruptions I shall be rid of, which I could not here. These croaking toads will fall off in a moment."[10]

Goodwin died in 1680 at the age of eighty. His remains were buried in Bunhill Fields.

The Vanity of Thoughts

Edmund Calamy (1671–1732) once said of Goodwin, "It is evident from his writings that he studied not words, but things. His style is plain and familiar; but very diffuse, homely, and tedious."[11] To be sure, Goodwin can be

---

9. Reid, *Memoirs of the Westminster Divines*, 1:338.

10. William S. Barker, *Puritan Profiles: 54 Puritans Personalities Drawn Together by the Westminster Assembly* (Ross-shire, Scotland: Mentor, 1996), 75.

11. Beeke and Pederson, *Meet the Puritans*, 274–75.

challenging to read. This is one reason modernizations of his books are so helpful for today's readers.

First published in 1638, Goodwin's *Vanity of Thoughts* is one of his earliest and shortest books. It is characterized by four traits.

First, it is *brief*. Goodwin is not known for brevity. Cotton Mather (1663–1728) humorously said that Goodwin "often soars like an eagle; perhaps, you would have been content, if sometimes a little more concisely."[12] But unlike many of Goodwin's treatises, this is a short book that you can easily read in two or three sittings.

Second, it is *convicting*. In this exposé of the human heart, Goodwin shows how the vanity of thoughts consists in our reluctance to think good thoughts (chapter 3); along with foolish, sinful, and curious thoughts; thoughts that make provision for the flesh; and vain imaginations (chapters 4 and 5). Goodwin combines his piercing application of Scripture with clear definitions and simple illustrations. The result, for any attentive reader, will be a deeper insight into the inner world of his mind and heart, and—by God's grace—a deeper repentance from sinful thoughts.

Third, this book is also *practical*. This is especially seen in the final two chapters of the book, where Goodwin specifies two practical uses of these considerations and then eight remedies against vain thoughts. Do not

---

12. Barker, *Puritan Profiles*, 77.

read these sections too quickly. Take time to ponder and reflect.

Finally, this book is *hopeful*. Goodwin is known for his deep grasp of the gospel and his Christ-centeredness, seen especially in his books *Christ the Mediator* and *Christ Set Forth*. While *The Vanity of Thoughts* has a more practical focus, his careful distinctions will help believers distinguish between the annoying *presence* of vain thoughts and the willing *embrace* of them in their hearts. This can greatly help the Christian with a sensitive conscience who is discouraged by troubling or sinful thoughts. And do not miss this note of gospel hope in chapter 6: "Consider your thoughts that you might be humbled. But, for all their multitude, do not be discouraged. For God has more thoughts of mercy than you have of rebellion."

A Note on the Editing

This version of *The Vanity of Thoughts* is a thorough modernization for contemporary readers. Archaic words have been replaced with modern synonyms. Metaphors, idioms, and illustrations have been clarified, updated, or amended as needed. Scripture references have been clarified, added, or included in footnotes for easy reference. Allusions to classical literature have been documented. The book has been broken down into seven chapters with clear subheadings, and an appendix has been added, entitled "How Thoughts Reveal Our Hearts," adapted from a section in *The Work of the Holy Ghost in Our Salvation*, found in volume 6 of Goodwin's *Works*.

My hope is that you will find this little book helpful both in understanding the vital importance of your thought life and in bringing every thought captive to the lordship of Jesus Christ.

—Brian G. Hedges

Introduction

O Jerusalem, wash thine heart from wickedness,
that thou mayest be saved. How long shall thy vain
thoughts lodge within thee?
                                                    —Jeremiah 4:14

In these words, Jeremiah compares the heart to a guest-house built with many large rooms in which are lodged multitudes of guests. Prior to conversion, all the vain, frivolous, lustful, profane, and immoral thoughts have free and open access to the heart. These thoughts have run riot all day. The unconverted heart is an open house to them, willingly giving them welcome and entertainment. It accompanies these thoughts, travels the world to feed these thoughts with pleasures, lodges and harbors them. And like unruly philanderers and rakish revelers, they lodge and party day and night, defiling the rooms they lodge in with their loathsome filth and vomit.

The Lord says, "How long shall they lodge in your heart while I 'stand at the door, and knock' (Rev. 3:20) with my Spirit, my Son, and my caravan of graces and cannot find admittance?" This house (the heart) must be washed from all this filthiness. "Wash thine heart from wickedness" (Jer. 4:14). Notice that the house is not only to be swept from gross evils but also washed. For in Matthew 12:43–44, the unclean spirit reenters into the house that is swept of obvious evils but was not thoroughly washed and cleansed of those deeper defilements that stick closer to the heart and are incorporated and wrought into the spirit.

But these vain, unruly guests must be kicked out the door without any warning or delay. They have stayed long enough—too long, in fact. How long? As the apostle says, "For the time past of our life may suffice us to have wrought the will of the Gentiles, when we walked in lasciviousness, lusts, excess of wine, revellings, banquetings, and abominable idolatries" (1 Peter 4:3). They must no longer lodge in your heart.

In conversion, it is not that this house (the soul) is to be pulled down, but only that these guests are to be turned out. And though they cannot be completely kept out—for they will still enter while we are in these houses of clay—yet they must not lodge; they must not remain as guests. So, if thoughts of anger and revenge come in the morning or during the day, they must be kicked out by nightfall. "Be ye angry, and sin not: let not the sun go down upon your wrath" (Eph. 4:26). Turn away angry thoughts, or you may find yourself lodging an even worse guest: "Neither give place to the devil" (v. 27)! "Then goeth he, and taketh with himself seven other spirits more wicked than himself, and they enter in and dwell there: and the last *state* of that man is worse than the first" (Matt. 12:45). And if unclean thoughts offer to come to bed with you when you lie down, do not let them lodge with you.

In other words, it is not what thoughts pass through your hearts but those which lodge or dwell in your hearts that shows your true repentance. Many good thoughts and emotions may pass like strangers through a bad man's heart. In the same way, multitudes of vain thoughts can make a highway through a believer's heart, disturbing him in his good duties with knocks and interruptions and break-ins. But these thoughts do not lodge there. They are not nurtured or harbored.

My plan in this book is to show the wickedness and the vanity of the heart by nature, particularly the vanity of thoughts. To expound this, I chose this text as my starting point. But I confess, this is a vast subject! To fully expose all the vanities of our thoughts would require us to travel the whole world. It was the task of Solomon, the wisest of men, to take a survey and give an account of all the vanity that abounds in all the creatures. This was the fruit of his study and labor. But the vanities of our thoughts are even greater. This little world shows even more variety of vanities than the great. For if it was through our thoughts that creation itself was subjected to vanity (Rom. 8:20), then our thoughts are even more subjected to it.

In handling this, we will consider: the nature of thoughts (chapter 1), the meaning of vanity (chapter 2), the nature of vain thoughts (chapters 3–5), the practical uses of these considerations (chapter 6) and the remedy against vain thoughts (chapter 7).

CHAPTER 1

The Nature of Thoughts

First, we must consider what is meant by *thoughts*, especially as they are the intended subject of this book—for it is necessary to set limits on this vast subject.

By *thoughts*, the Scriptures include all the internal acts of any faculty of the human mind, including all the reasonings, consultations, purposes, resolutions, intentions, goals, desires, and cares of the human mind in contrast to our external words and actions. In Isaiah 66:18 all human acts are divided into these two categories: "I know their works and their thoughts." Things that are transacted within the mind are called thoughts, while those things that manifest themselves in actions are called works.

In Genesis 6:5 we read of "every imagination of the thoughts"—all the creatures the mind frames within itself, purposes, desires, and so forth (as is noted in the margin)—are evil.[1] *Thoughts* are here understood as

---

1. Goodwin is referring to the marginal note for Genesis 6:5 in

all that comes within the mind (as in Ezek. 11:5), and this is also how we commonly understand the word. For example, to remember a man is to "think" of him (see Gen. 40:14). To have purposed a thing, we say "I thought to do it." To take care of business is to "take thought" (1 Sam. 9:5).

And the reason all these examples may be called thoughts is because all affections, desires, and purposes are indeed stirred up by thoughts. They are bred, fueled, and nourished by the thoughts. For not a single thought passes through the mind without stirring some affection of fear, joy, care, grief, and so forth.

Although *thoughts* have such a broad scope here, yet I do not intend to presently handle thoughts in the broadest sense. Instead, I must confine myself to the vanity of that which is more properly called the thinking, meditating, considering power of man, which is in his understanding or spirit. This is the subject at hand: thoughts not only in contrast to works but also in contrast to purposes and intentions. For just as the soul is distinguished from spirit in Hebrews 4:12, so also are thoughts distinguished from intentions. And in Job 20:2–3, "thoughts" are appropriated to the spirit of understanding.

---

the 1611 King James Version: "The Hebr. word signifieth not only the imagination, but also the purposes and desires."

To narrow things down even more, by *understanding*, I mean to speak of it not generally as comprising all thoughts, reasonings, or deliberations in our actions, but rather will confine this book to those musings in the speculative faculty of the mind.

The best way I can express the meaning of thoughts to you is like this: by *thoughts* I mean those first simple notions conceived in the mind, or those perceptions, imaginings, and meditations which arise in the mind, which the understanding with the help of the imagination frames within itself. These are the thoughts by which your minds ponder, pore over, and muse upon things. I mean that inner dialogue in our minds with those things we know (Prov. 6:22); I mean those same conversations, interviews, and chats that the mind has with the things it lets into it—the things we fear and love. For the mind makes all these things its companions and by its thoughts converses with them and has a thousand notions about them. This is what I mean by *thoughts*.

For there is a reasoning, deliberating, determining faculty by which we reason and discuss things and continually ask ourselves, "What shall we do?" This is like an inner chamber, the private council of the heart. But there is also a more outward lodging, a chamber which entertains all who come. This is the thinking, musing, meditating faculty, which suggests the raw material for deliberations, consultations, and reasonings, and holds

objects up for our consideration and entertains all that
come to speak with any of our affections.

I will add that we are considering those thoughts
which the mind frames within itself. For so the Scriptures
express the origin of thoughts, the manner of their rising,
in Proverbs 6:14:

> Perversity is in his heart,
> He devises evil continually,
> He sows discord. (NKJV)

He devises or forges evil the way a smith forges iron and
hammers it out. And the thoughts are the materials of
this perversity in us. Upon all things presented to us, the
mind conceives some thoughts or imaginations about
them. Thoughts, like lusts, are conceived within (James
1:14–15). As Isaiah 59:4–5 says, "They conceive mischief,
and bring forth iniquity. They hatch cockatrice' eggs,
and weave the spider's web." And he gives an example in
verse 7: "Their thoughts are thoughts of iniquity." For
thoughts are spun out of our own hearts, and eggs are of
our own laying, though they may be occasioned by the
external objects presented to us.

I say this to distinguish our own thoughts from those
that are injected and cast in solely from without. These
are children of another's begetting and are often laid
out of doors. Such are blasphemous thoughts cast in by
Satan. In these, if the soul is merely passive (as the word
"buffet" implies in 2 Cor. 12:7), then they are not your
own thoughts, but Satan's. It is like when a man shares

his room with another and hears him swear and curse and cannot get away from him. Such thoughts, if they are only from without, do not defile a man. For nothing defiles except that which comes from within (Matt. 15:18–19) or which the heart has begotten upon it by the devil (such as thoughts of impurity), in which though he is the father, yet the heart is the mother and womb. These affect the heart just as natural children do their parents.

And this is how we may distinguish these from one another: when we have a soft heart and an inward love for them, so that our hearts do (as it were) kiss the child, then they are our own thoughts. And when the heart broods upon these eggs, they are our own thoughts, even if suggested from without.

In addition, sometimes, when the soul is passive but Satan casts in thoughts which we would never own, when rather than begetting thoughts in our hearts he forces thoughts upon us without our consent, yet such thoughts may be punishments for neglecting our thoughts and allowing them to wander. Or they may be punishments for neglecting the good motions of the Spirit, whom we resist and grieve, so that He chastens us and allows us to be frightened that we may learn not to neglect Him or harbor vanity.

Finally, I will add this qualification: we are here considering those thoughts which the mind, in and by itself or with the help of the imagination, conceives and entertains. For there are never any perceptions of things in our imaginations that are not at the same time reflected in our understanding. If you place two mirrors opposite one another, an object reflected in one will be seen in the other. In the same way, the objects in our imaginations are reflected in our thoughts.

CHAPTER 2

The Meaning of Vanity

Second, we must consider the meaning of *vanity*. If you take it in all the accepted meanings of the word, it is true that our thoughts are vain.

Senses of the Word *Vanity*

Sometimes vanity is taken for unprofitableness, for example, in Ecclesiastes 1:2: "Vanity of vanities, saith the Preacher, vanity of vanities; all is vanity." Why? Because they are without profit: "What profit hath a man of all his labour which he taketh under the sun?" (v. 3). Such are our thoughts by nature. The wisest of them will not uphold us in any situation—in time of need, temptation, distress of conscience, the day of death, or judgment; 1 Corinthians 2:6 says that all the wisdom of the wise comes to nothing. "The heart of the wicked is worth little" (Prov. 10:20)—not a penny for them all.

In contrast, the thoughts of a godly man are his treasure—out of the good treasure of his heart he brings them forth (Matt. 12:35). He mints them, and they are laid up as his riches. "How precious are they" (see Ps. 139:17), he says of our thoughts of God. When God is the object of our thoughts, they are precious.

Vanity is sometimes taken for lightness. Psalm 62:9 uses the phrase "lighter than vanity." And of whom is this spoken? Of men. And if anything in men is lighter than anything else, it is their thoughts, which swim in the uppermost parts, which float at the top, and are as the scum of the heart.

Take Belshazzar, king of the Chaldeans. When all his best, wisest, deepest, most solid thoughts were put in the scales and weighed, they were found too light (Dan. 5:27).[1]

Vanity is also a synonym for folly. In Proverbs 12:11, "vain persons" are equivalent to men who are "void of understanding." Such are our thoughts. Among the other evils which are said to come "out of the heart" is foolishness (Mark 7:21–22). This word can refer to the nonsensical thoughts of madmen or fools: without purpose, use, or even clear cause and effect.

Vanity also refers to constancy and frailty. Therefore, vanity is compared to a shadow in Psalm 144:4. Such are our thoughts, fleeting and perishing like bubbles—"his thoughts perish" (Ps. 146:4).

---

1. See the full account of this remarkable story in Daniel 5:1–30.

Last, when it is said that our thoughts are vain it means indeed that they are wicked and sinful. Vanity in the text is here yoked with wickedness. And vain men are identified with the sons of Belial in 2 Chronicles 13:7.[2]

And such are our thoughts by nature. "The thought of foolishness is sin" (Prov. 24:9). And therefore a man is to be humbled for a proud thought. As Proverbs 30:32 says, "If thou hast done foolishly in lifting up thyself, or if thou hast thought evil, lay thine hand upon thy mouth." And in Job 40:4, this laying the hand upon the mouth is taken for the humility of a man who is vile in his own eyes.

And because this is the sense I chiefly must insist upon in handling the vanity of thoughts (and also because men usually think that thoughts are free of guilt), I will prove that vain thoughts are sins. This is the only doctrine raised.[3]

---

2. "Belial" is a Hebrew epithet that probably has the literal meaning of useless or worthless, although the derivation is not clear. The phrase "sons of Belial" in Scripture generally refers to the wicked or foolish. Belial is also used as a proper name for Satan in the New Testament. For more, see "Belial" in D. R. W. Wood, I. H. Marshall, A. R. Millard, J. I. Packer, and D. J. Wiseman, eds., *New Bible Dictionary*, 3rd ed. (Downers Grove, Ill.: InterVarsity Press, 1996), 127.

3. Goodwin was following the typical Puritan approach to preaching by first setting forth the doctrine (or main teaching point) of a passage, and then following this with the uses (or application). For the uses, see chapter 6.

Why Vain Thoughts Are Sins

The law judges the thoughts (Heb. 4:12) and rebukes a man for them (1 Cor. 14:25). Therefore, vain thoughts are a transgression of the law. This is why Christ rebuked the Pharisees for their ill thoughts (Matt. 9:4). And this shows the excellency of the law, which even reaches the thoughts.

Thoughts are capable of pardon, and must be pardoned, or we cannot be saved (Acts 8:22). This shows the greatness of God's compassion, seeing that thoughts are so infinite.

Thoughts are to be repented of. In fact, repentance is expressed as beginning with the thoughts, for Isaiah 55:7 says, "Let the wicked forsake his way, and the unrighteous man his thoughts." And a genuine, thorough work upon the soul leads to the subduing of the thoughts, as in 2 Corinthians 10:4–5: "Bringing into captivity every thought to the obedience of Christ." This argues that our thoughts are naturally rebellious and contrary to grace. And it also shows the power of grace, which is able to rule and subdue such a great army as our thoughts, commanding them all—as someday it will do when we are perfectly holy.

Thoughts defile the man. But nothing defiles a man except sin. "Out of the heart proceed evil thoughts.... These are the things which defile a man" (Matt. 15:19–20).

Evil thoughts are an abomination to the Lord, who hates nothing but sin and whose pure eyes cannot endure to behold iniquity (Hab. 1:13). As good meditations are acceptable to the Lord (Ps. 19:14), so, by the rule of opposites, bad thoughts are abominable.

Thoughts hinder all the good we should do and spoil our best performances of duty. Vain thoughts draw the heart away with them, so that when a man should draw near to God, his heart (because of his thoughts) is far from Him (Isa. 29:13). A man's heart goes after his covetousness. When he should be listening to the prophet's words, his thoughts run after covetousness (Ezek. 33:31). Nothing but sin could separate; sin and enmity against God is what estranges us from Him.

Our thoughts are the first movers that propose all the evil that is within us. For they make the motion and bring the heart and object together. Thoughts cater to our lusts, holding up the object of desire, until the heart has played the adulterer with it and committed folly. This is so in mental impurity, as well as in other sinful desires. Thoughts hold up the images of the gods they create, which the heart then bows down to worship. Thoughts present honor, riches, and beauty to our hearts until the heart worships them, even the things themselves are absent.

CHAPTER 3

Reluctance toward Good Thoughts

We come now to the specific features which consist in the vanity of the thinking, meditating power of the mind. I will explain this in two ways: first, in showing the inability and reluctance of the mind to think of that which is good; second, in showing how ready the mind is to think of vain and evil things.

The reluctance of the mind to think of that which is good is seen in four things.

To Draw Holy Thoughts from Ordinary Life

This reluctance is seen first of all in the inability, ordinarily and naturally, to raise and extract holy and useful thoughts and considerations from the ordinary occurrences and occasions of life. When the mind is sanctified, it is quick to do this. A sanctified heart, in whose affections true grace has been kindled, draws holy, sweet, and useful meditations out of all God's dealings with him—all that he sees and hears, all the objects put into his thoughts. This is the sanctified heart's usual, natural inclination.

We see this in Christ our Savior throughout the Gospels. All that He heard from others and all the occurrences of His life were occasions for His heavenly meditations. When He came to a well, He spoke of the living water (John 4:10, 14). Many examples could be given. In His thoughts, He translated the book of creation into the book of grace. His philosophy was truly divinity because He saw God in everything—and in everything raised up His heart to thankfulness and praise. Adam, in his innocence, did this as well.

And our minds, insofar as they are sanctified, will do the same. As the philosopher's stone turns all metals into gold, and as the bee sucks honey out of every flower, and a good stomach digests sweet and wholesome nourishment from what it eats, so does a holy heart, so far as it is sanctified, convert and digest all things into useful thoughts.

We see this in Psalm 107. This psalm gives many instances of God's providence, the wonderful works which doth for the sons of men. These include deliverances at sea where men see His wonders, deliverance to captives, and more. But throughout the psalm, the refrain is "Oh that men would praise the LORD for his goodness, and for his wonderful works to the children of men!" (vv. 8, 15, 21, 31). Then, after all these examples, he concludes that though others pass over such things with slight, ordinary thoughts, "the righteous shall see it, and rejoice" (v. 42). In other words, he extracts comforting thoughts out of everything, and this becomes to him a matter of joy. "Whoso is wise, and will observe these things" (v. 43) — that is, will make holy observations out of these things. For out of a principle of wisdom, he understands God's goodness in all things, and thus his heart is raised to thoughts of praise, thankfulness, and obedience.

Now, compare this with Psalm 92, a psalm made for the Sabbath, when in imitation of God, who viewed His works on the seventh day, we are, on our Lord's Day, to raise holy thoughts of praise to His glory as we observe His works. This is what the psalmist does. "How great are thy works!" he says (v. 5). In contrast, "A brutish man knoweth not; neither doth a fool understand this" (v. 6). That is, being brutish like a beast and having no sanctified principle of wisdom within him, he looks no further than a beast into all the works of God and daily occurrences. He may look upon blessings as things provided by God for man's delight, but he seldom extracts holy, spiritual, or useful thoughts from them. He lacks the art of doing so.

Or consider the case of injuries received from others. When this happens, what do our thoughts draw out of these wrongs, except thoughts of revenge? We meditate on how to pay back those who hurt us with vengeance. But notice how quickly David's mind draws other thoughts from Shimei's cursing in 2 Samuel 16:11–12: "Let him alone, and let him curse; for the LORD hath bidden him. It may be that the LORD will look on mine affliction, and that the LORD will requite me good for his cursing this day." This may prove to be a sign of God's favor. The Lord may requite good for it.

Or when we see judgments fall upon others, we are like Job's friends. We entertain severe thoughts of censure against our brother. But a godly man whose mind is greatly sanctified raises other thoughts from these judgments. "A wicked man hardeneth his face: but as for the upright, he considereth his way" (Prov. 21:29, KJV marginal reading).

And when outward mercies befall us, we are prone to think of the ease wealth will bring us. "Soul, thou hast much goods laid up for many years; take thine ease, eat, drink, and be merry" (Luke 12:19). But then when judgments befall us, we are prone to be filled with thoughts of complaint, and with fears and cares about how to escape. But what were Job's first thoughts upon the news of losing everything? "The LORD gave, and the LORD hath taken away; blessed be the name of the LORD" (Job 1:21).

These are the kinds of thoughts which a good heart is prone to and naturally raises for its own use in all the diverse situations of life. But to whatever degree our thoughts are barren of such thoughts, to that degree they are vain thoughts.

To Set One's Mind upon God

The vanity and sinfulness of the mind is seen in a reluctance to entertain holy thoughts and to begin setting itself to think about God and the things belonging to our peace. Our minds are as loath to think of God as schoolboys are to study their books or get busy doing their lessons. Instead, their heads are full of play.

In the same way, our minds are loath to seriously consider solemn thoughts about God or death. Men are as reluctant to think about death as criminals are to think about execution for their crimes. And men are as reluctant to think about God as criminals are of their judge.

Men are also reluctant to think over their own actions, to review them, to read the blurred writing of their hearts and commune with them at night at the end of the day (as David did in Ps. 77:6).[1] They are as loath to do this as schoolboys are to parse their lessons and correct their mistakes in Latin! Like in Job 21:14, they say to God, "Depart from us; for we desire not knowledge of thy ways." They do not want to think of Him or know Him.

And, therefore, our minds, like a bad stomach, are nauseated with the very scent of good things and soon vomit them up again: "They did not like to retain God in their knowledge" (Rom. 1:28).

---

1. In earlier editions of *The Vanity of Thoughts*, the reference is to Psalm 119:59: "I thought on my ways, and turned my feet unto thy testimonies."

Let us go and try to raise up our souls at any time to holy meditations, to think of what we have heard, or what we have done, or what it is our duty to do, and we shall find our minds, like the pegs of an instrument, slipping between our fingers as we are winding them up. They fall down suddenly again before we are aware of it. Indeed, you will find that you strive to stay away from things that occasion such thoughts, even as men cross the street when they see someone they do not wish to speak with. Indeed, men do not dare to spend time alone because they are afraid such thoughts should return to them.

Even the best of men are glad to find an excuse to distract their minds from what is good. But when thinking of vain, earthly things, we think the time passes too fast, the clock strikes too soon, and before we know it, the hours have passed away.

To Sustain Good Thoughts

The vanity and sinfulness of the mind appears even in the godly, in that when they entertain good thoughts, their minds will not sustain long concentration upon them. There are some things upon which we can easily concentrate. We thus dwell long upon them. The thoughts are therefore called (in Hebrew), the "possessions of the heart" (Job 17:11, KJV marginal reading). The heart dwells upon thoughts that are pleasant. Indeed, it is so focused on them that they often hinder our sleep. As it is said of wicked men, they cannot sleep for multitude of thoughts (Eccl. 5:12).[2] Or, as Solomon says in Proverbs 16:30, "He shutteth his eyes to devise froward things." That is, he is deeply attentive, poring over his plots, for as a person closes his eyes when he wants to think deeply or concentrate, so it is expressed here.

But let the mind be occupied instead with good things, things belonging to our peace, and how unsteady it is! These things should draw forth the mind's intention. For the more excellent the object is, the stronger our intention should be. God is the most glorious, most alluring object our minds can think upon. Thoughts of Him should therefore swallow up all other thoughts, as not worthy to be seen the same day with Him. But I appeal to your experience. Are not your thoughts of Him most unsteady? They are like someone who looks upon a star through a telescope but holds it with a shaky hand.

It takes a long time for us to bring our minds to know Him, to place our eyes upon Him. And when we have, how do our hands shake and every so often lose sight of Him! Even when we are seriously engaged with Him and when we should keep all other things out of our minds, not daring to admit them until we have concluded our converse with God, yet how many cracks and crevices are found in the heart through which other thoughts come in! Then our minds leave God and follow these

---

2. The KJV says, "The abundance of the rich will not suffer him to sleep." Though this likely refers to an abundance of wealth, Goodwin seems to take it as an abundance or multitude of thoughts.

other things, going after covetousness (Ezek. 33:31), our reputation, and so forth. For example, when we are hearing the Word, how often do our minds run out of the church and then come in again, so that we miss half of what was said! Or when we attend to our work, which God bids us to do with all our might (Eccl. 9:10), our minds, like idle bums or neglectful servants, even though sent on serious business, yet take detours to watch a sport or chase rabbits or butterflies that fly about us!

This is why when we come to pray, Christ bids us to "watch and pray" (Mark 13:33). We should, as it were, place a guard at every door so that no one comes in to disturb us and distract us from prayer. But how often does the heart nod off, fall asleep, and run into the world of dreams! Indeed, distractions are so natural to us when we attend to our holy duties, that as coughs and sneezes come from those who are sick and weak, though they are hardly aware of it, so do worldly thoughts come from us. We are carried away from the stream of good thoughts into some little creek before we are aware of it.

To Think Good Things in Due Season

The vanity of the mind further appears in that when people do think good things, yet they fail to do so in due season. The goodness of our thoughts, like words, lies in their place and order: "A word fitly spoken is like apples of gold in pictures of silver" (Prov. 25:11). And as a man is to bring forth actions as fruits in due season (Ps. 1:3), so also the buds of our thoughts.

But the vanity of the mind is seen in thinking about some good things out of season. For example, when you are praying, you should have not only no worldly thoughts distract you but no thoughts other than prayerful thoughts. But there you are praying, when suddenly you have an idea for a sermon. So also in hearing the Word. A man shall often have good thoughts that are different from the present subject. Or when someone is starting to pray, he suddenly remembers something important he had forgotten, and this diverts and distracts him.

This misplacing of even good thoughts is yet another result of vanity in the mind. If those thoughts came at another time, they would be welcome. But we find our minds ready to spend thoughts on anything rather than what God is presently calling us to. When we go to hear a sermon, we find that we could willingly be reading or happily searching our hearts. But at another time when we called to these things, we are most unwilling to do them! We could be content to run wild over the fields of meditations on miscellaneous good thoughts rather than be tied to the task at hand or keep to the path set before us.

But for Adam in his innocence and for Christ, there was never a single thought misplaced. Though their thoughts were as many as the stars, yet they marched in their orbits and stayed in their proper place. But our thoughts are like meteors. They dance up and down within us. And this disorder is a vanity and sin, though the matter of the thoughts themselves are good. In acting, the person with the best part is not always the first on stage—he must instead come on cue. In printing, though the letters are never so fair, they will make no sense unless rightly composed and placed in the proper order. In the army, soldiers must never break their ranks. So it is with our thoughts. There is a promise to the righteous man that (as some read it) his thoughts should be ordered (Prov. 16:3).

These four things show us the sinfulness of our thoughts in their reluctance and disorder in thinking about that which is good.

CHAPTER 4

Evil Thoughts

Having considered the vanity of the mind in its reluctance to consider what is good, we now turn to discover how vanity appears in our thoughts concerning what is evil. It is not here expected or even possible to consider the many diverse ways such vain thoughts run through man's heart. I will only insist on the general categories, to which some more particular examples can be added as a taste for the rest.

Foolish Thoughts

The vanity of thoughts is seen in that which Christ calls "foolishness" (Mark 7:22)—that is, such thoughts as fools and madmen have. This is seen in the unsettled wantonness and restlessness of the mind. Its thoughts, like mercury, cannot be fixed. As Solomon says, "The eyes of a fool are in the ends of the earth" (Prov. 17:24). They run up and down from one end of the earth to the other, shooting and streaking this way and that, like meteors in the night sky. The mind of man is indeed nimble and thus able to run from one end of the earth to the other, and this is its strength and excellence. Yet God would not have such a mind darting here and there, but rather steadfastly directing all our thought straight to His glory, our salvation, and the good of others.

He gave the mind this nimbleness, that it might quickly turn from evil, even the first appearance of evil. We are to walk in the ways to which God calls us. Therefore, every thought, as well as every action, is a step, and these steps should be steady. As the apostle says, "Make straight paths for your feet" (Heb. 12:13). Do not turn to the right hand nor to the left until you come to your journey's end.

But our thoughts at best are as unrestrained spaniels, who though they accompany their master and come with him to their journey's end, yet run after every bird and wildly pursue every flock of sheep they see. This unsteadiness arises from a curse on the mind of man—like Cain, who was driven from the presence of the Lord (Gen. 4:14–16), making us vagabonds whose eyes are in the ends of the earth.

This foolishness is also seen in the disjointedness of our thoughts, which often hang together like a rope made of sand. This is especially evident in dreams, but not only then but also when we are awake and try to set ourselves to be most serious, while our thoughts jingle and ring backward! Our thoughts are like restless boys, who, when they take pens in their hands, scribble down broken words that have no sequence or meaning. If you were to look at a written transcript of your thoughts, you would find as much nonsense as you would find in a madman's speech.

This madness and distemper have been in the mind since the fall (though it is not as evident in our words, because we know better). But if notes were taken of our thoughts, we would find them so to be such vagrant, wandering thoughts that we would not know how they came in, where they came from, or where they are going. But as God does all things in weight, number, and measure, so His image does within us, so far as it is renewed.

And by reason of the folly, unsettledness, and disjointedness of our thoughts, we are often unable to bring our thoughts to a good result. Far from perfecting our thoughts, we waste away time in thinking of nothing. And as Seneca says of men's lives, they are like ships tossed up and down at sea that have been tossed much but have sailed little, so the same may be said of the thoughts.[1] Or as when men make imperfect dashes and

---

1. Lucius Annaeus Seneca (ca. 4 BC–AD 65) was a statesman and Stoic philosopher in ancient Rome. Goodwin's reference is to Seneca's essay "De Brevitate Vitae" ("On the Shortness of Life"). Here is the quotation: "For what if you should think that that man had had a long voyage who had been caught by a fierce storm as soon as he left harbour, and, swept hither and thither by a succession of winds that raged from different quarters, had been driven in a circle around the same course? Not much voyaging did he have, but much tossing about." Seneca, *Moral Essays, Volume II: De Consolatione ad*

write nonsense they are said to scribble but do not really write, so in these follies and independencies, we wander and lose ourselves. We do not think.

Sinful Thoughts

In contrast, our thoughts are too fixed on sinful objects, especially when there arises a strong lust or violent passion. Our thoughts then run so far into sinful objects that they cannot be diverted or pulled back again. And this is another case of vanity in the mind.

For our thoughts and the faculty of understanding were ordained to moderate, dispel, and cool off our stirring passions—to rule and govern them. But now our thoughts are themselves subjected to our affections; they add fuel to the fire, making them boil and blaze even more. And although our thoughts first stir up our fears, joys, desires, and so forth, yet these affections, once stirred, fix our thoughts to those objects. They have such a hold on our minds that we cannot loosen them again. This is why Christ says to His disciples, "Why are ye troubled? and why do thoughts arise in your hearts?" (Luke 24:38). For disturbances in the affections cause thoughts to ascend in the mind like fumes.

Marciam. De Vita Beata. De Otio. De Tranquillitate Animi. De Brevitate Vitae. De Consolatione ad Polybium. De Consolatione ad Helviam, trans. John W. Basore, Loeb Classical Library, no. 254 (Cambridge, Mass.: Harvard University Press, 1932), 308.

For example, if a passion of fear is strong, it conjures up multitudes of ghostly thoughts that haunt us, following us wherever we go. We cannot conjure them down again, but instead hide our eyes. Like a man pursued by his own thoughts, "thine heart shall meditate terror" (Isa. 33:18). Or when sorrow fills the heart, it makes us study the cross that descends upon us, though forgetting it would ease the mind! But a man's passions make his thoughts to analyze and scrutinize his sorrow, to say it over and over again, to so learn it by heart as if never to forget it again. Or take love and desire. When they are strong, whatever their object—whether honor, beauty, or riches—it gets our thoughts working to view the object of desire from every angle, from top to bottom; to observe every part and circumstance that makes it amiable to us, as if to draw a picture of it. Or when joy is full, we focus on the thing we rejoice in, read it over and over as we read a book we like, marking every page.

Indeed, we are so inordinate in this that we often cannot sleep. "The abundance of the rich will not suffer him to sleep" (Eccl. 5:12) because of the multitude of thoughts in his head. Consider how thoughts trouble the Nebuchadnezzars of the world![2] As Proverbs 4:16 says, "For they sleep not, except they have done mischief." If their desires remain unsatisfied, their thoughts are disturbed, like willful children by their crying.

---

2. See Daniel 2:1.

So often these thoughts, which men consider to be free, instead prove to be the greatest bondage and torment to them in the world. They hinder sleep, the nurse of nature. They eat away and live upon the heart that bred them. They weary their spirits, so that rather than saying, "My bed shall comfort me" (Job 7:13) by putting a pause to the thoughts and sad discourses he has when awake, they haunt the man, they terrify him (Job 7:14). A man cannot lay his thoughts aside as he does his clothes. And when men die, their thoughts follow them to hell and torment them even more there. Your thoughts will be one of the greatest executioners there, even the worm that dies not (Mark 9:48).

Curious Thoughts

The vanity of the mind also appears in curiosity, a longing and itching to know things that do not concern us. Curiosity delights to be fed with such things. Test this out with young students, whose chief work lies in this shop. How many precious thoughts are spent in this way! The apostle rebukes this curiosity after knowledge and exhorts us to avoid "the profane and idle babblings and contradictions of what is falsely called knowledge" (1 Tim. 6:20 NKJV) and those who are curious about things they have not seen (Col. 2:18). He calls the result of such thoughts "old wives' fables" (1 Tim. 4:7) because as fables please old wives, so do these thoughts please their minds. Like expectant mothers with their strange cravings for some unusual, rare food, these men are not content with the wonders of God discovered in the depth of His Word and works. Instead, they launch into another sea, into a world of their own making, and sail with pleasure. So many of the schoolmen[3] did in some of their speculations, spending their precious wits in framing curious webs spun from their own bowels.

For another example, think of those who have leisure for much reading. They should ballast their hearts with the Word and take in those more precious words, wisdom, and sound knowledge in order to profit themselves and others. This would build up their souls and enable them to serve others. But what do their curious fancies carry them to, but books of plays, jeering satires, fictional romances, and other tales—the curious needlework of idle brains! They load their heads with apes and peacocks' feathers instead of pearls and precious stones.[4] As Solomon says, "The heart of him that

---

3. "Schoolmen" refers to the Scholastic theologians of the medieval church, such as Thomas Aquinas (1225–1274), Duns Scotus (ca. 1266–1308), and William of Ockham (ca. 1287–1347). Goodwin here compares them to spiders who spin curious webs of their own making. While the Reformers and Puritans could be critical of the Scholastic theologians, this should not imply a wholesale rejection of everything they taught. For a comprehensive study of the complex relationship between Scholasticism and the Reformation, see Matthew Barrett, *The Reformation as Renewal: Retrieving the One, Holy, Catholic, Apostolic Church* (Grand Rapids: Zondervan Academic, 2023).

4. An allusion to 1 Kings 10:22, where Solomon's navy is said to

hath understanding seeketh knowledge: but the mouth of fools feedeth on foolishness" (Prov. 15:14). Their ears and eyes are pleased by foolish discourses, which are really just purveyors that supply food for the thoughts. Like chameleons, these men live on air and wind.[5]

Others, out of mere curiosity, listen to news from all over the world, all to please their thoughts with the froth of foolish men's mouths and please themselves with talking, thinking, and hearing about it. I do not condemn all in this. Some have good intentions and can make use of it, as did Nehemiah, who inquired how things went at Jerusalem so as to rejoice with, mourn with, and pray for God's people. He sought news that he might shape his prayers accordingly. But I do condemn that itch of curiosity within them when it is sought to merely please their imaginations, which delights much in new things, even though they are not personally concerned in them. Such were those in Athens (Acts 17:21). Some people constantly long to learn of issues and events. They make it part of their happiness to study the world more than their own hearts and the affairs of their own callings. They take

have brought to Jerusalem gold, silver, and ivory, as well as apes and peacocks.

5. In the seventeenth century, it was commonly assumed that chameleons did not eat food but lived on air. This assumption is also seen in lines from Shakespeare's *Two Gentlemen of Verona*: "Ay, but hearken, sir; though the chameleon Love can feed on the air, I am one that am nourished by my victuals, and would fain have meat" (Act 2, Scene 1).

politics as their text to study and preach upon wherever they go! I speak of those who do not lay to heart the miseries of Christ's church nor help them with their prayers.

A similar curiosity is seen in many who desire to know the secrets of others, though it would do them no good to know. They study men's actions and ends not to reform or do good to them, but to know, think, and muse upon them in solitude with pleasure. This is curiosity. It is properly a vanity of the faculty of thinking, which it mainly seeks to please. And it is indeed a great sin when many of men's most pleasing thoughts are spent on things that do not concern them. For the things we ought to know, and which do concern us, are themselves enough to take up all our thoughts. Nor do we have any thoughts to spare, for thoughts are precious things, the immediate fruits of an immortal nature. And God has given us power to form thoughts and use them in things that concern our own good, and that of our neighbors, and His glory. To not spend thoughts on these things is the greatest waste in the world. Examine what corn you have put in to grind, for God ought to have toll of all. "He that deviseth to do evil shall be called a mischievous person" (Prov. 24:8)— not only he who does a mischievous action, but he who devises it. And he makes it worse, for if every "thought of foolishness is sin" (Prov. 24:9), how much more the combination and conspiracy of wicked thoughts.

Fleshly Thoughts

There is a worse vanity than this suggested in Romans 13:14: taking thought to make provision for the flesh to fulfill the lusts thereof, to make projects for it. For thoughts are the caterers for our lusts and supply all their provision. Like caterers, thoughts search out the best markets, the best opportunities, the best bargains for credit, for honor, for riches, and so forth.

For example, does a man to desire to rise in reputation? His thoughts study the art of it. Men frame their own ladder to climb upward and invent ways to do it—though this often proves to be their own gallows, as with Haman.[6]

Would they be rich? What do they study but all the cheats and tricks of the world, all the ways of oppressing and defrauding, of going beyond their fellows and framing deals that make themselves the winners and others the losers. As Isaiah 32:7 says, the scoundrel's instruments "are evil: he deviseth wicked devices to destroy the poor with lying words."

Would a man undermine his opponent who stands in his way and hinders his reputation? He will dig a pit for his enemy in the night with his thoughts, plots, and schemes. As the Scripture puts it, he will dig deep to

---

6. A reference to Haman in the book of Esther, whose proud ambition eventually led to his own demise. See especially chapters 5–7.

hide his counsel, to harm in the end, so that his opponent will not know who hurt him.[7]

And this studied artifice, this deliberate villainy, is worse than all the former examples, for the plotting and devising in it is sin. This is why David's sin against Uriah is even worse than his adultery with Bathsheba. For in killing Uriah, David plotted and schemed; he took thought for it, but in the matter of Bathsheba, thoughts took him.

Imagination

The fifth example of vanity regarding evil is in the imagination. Here men represent sins in their thoughts and minds, enjoying pleasures of sin in their minds though not in reality, as they imagine themselves engaged in sinful practices which they do not have the outward opportunity to perform. The theologians call this *speculative wickedness*. This is evident in dreams, when imagination most plays its part and makes us believe we eat when we are hungry and drink when our souls are thirsty (Isa. 29:8).

But I am not merely speaking about the corruption of imagination in our dreams. It would be well if this speculative wickedness took place only "in the night"—as the apostle says of drunkenness (1 Thess. 5:7). But corrupt, distempered affections cast men into such dreams

---

7. See Psalm 35:7.

during the day, while they are awake. Then there are
filthy dreams that defile the flesh (Jude 8), even when
awake. For when their lusts desire to work, their imagination builds them a stage and they set their minds and
thoughts at work to entertain their filthy and impure
desires with shows and plays of their own making. Then
reason and the intention of the minds sit as spectators to
view their imaginations with pleasure till their thoughts
inwardly act out over their unclean desires, ambitious
projects, and whatever else they have a mind to.

This representation of sins in our thoughts does
three things: it makes the heart of man vain and empty;
it shows how our desires are impatient; and it reveals the
imagination to be sinful and corrupt.

These imaginations render the heart of man vain
and empty. This is evident, for the pleasures of sin in
the mind—when they are not fully, solidly, and substan-
tially enjoyed in reality—are but shadows. Imagination
casts upon sins a varnish of goodness that is not really in
them. That is why Agrippa and Bernice's pomp is called
a *phantasia*.[8] These things are shadows, but when men's
hearts take pleasure by enjoying them only in the imagination, when we please ourselves with bare thoughts of
them, this is but a shadow of a shadow! Like Ixion, the

---

8. *Phantasia* is the Greek word from which we get our word *fan-
tasy*. In Acts 25:23, it carries the sense of pomp or pageantry, but for
Goodwin the wordplay suggests the emptiness of such worldly displays of splendor.

soul embraces and commits adultery with only a cloud.[9] This is a vanity beyond all other vanities, making more vain than other creatures who, though "subject to vanity," do not yet reach to this.

This shows how impatient our desires are when they are kept from or interrupted in their pleasures. The soul is greedy when, kept from its desires and lacking the opportunities or means to act upon its lusts, it seeks instead to enjoy them through empty pictures drawn in the imagination.

This also reveals that our imaginations are exceedingly sinful and corrupt. An outward act of sin, when committed, is like an act of adultery with the creature. But representing sin in the thoughts is like an act of incest in which we defile our souls and spirits with imaginations and likeness born from our own minds, being the children of our own hearts.

---

9. In Greek mythology, Ixion, the king of Lapiths, lusted after Hera, the wife of Zeus. When Zeus discovered Ixion's adulterous intentions, he made a cloud (Nephele, from *nephos*, cloud) in the shape of Hera. Through the trickery of Zeus, Ixion copulated with Nephele. See Lucian, *Dialogues of the Dead. Dialogues of the Sea-Gods. Dialogues of the Gods. Dialogues of the Courtesans*, trans. M. D. MacLeod, Loeb Classical Library, no. 431 (Cambridge, Mass: Harvard University Press, 1961), 275–81.

CHAPTER 5

Sinful Imaginations

And yet, my brethren, the mind of man is full of such speculative enjoying of pleasures and acting over of sins! This is seen in four ways.

Things Present

Consider the comforts men presently have in their possession and what excellencies and endowments they have at their command. Men love to be alone to study and think of them. Even when they are kept from the present use of them, they are yet recounting them in their minds, surveying their happiness in these comforts, and applauding their hearts in their conditions.

Just as rich men who love money love to look at it and count it, so do men in adding up the comforts and privileges they enjoy, which other people lack. They consider how rich they are, how great, how they surpass others in possessions, abilities, and opportunities. But how much of the precious sand of our thoughts run out in doing this![1]

For an example, think of the rich man who kept an inventory in his heart: "Soul, thou hast much goods laid up for many years" (Luke 12:19). Or consider Haman, who counted up his honors and goods, talking of "the glory of his riches…and all the things wherein the king had promoted him" (Est. 5:11). We also see this in Nebuchadnezzar, who it seems was walking alone and talking to himself like a fool, saying, "Is not this great Babylon, that I have built for the house of the kingdom by the might of my power, and for the honour of my majesty?" (Dan. 4:30).

And just as men think thus upon their comforts, so they also think upon their excellencies, their learning, their wisdom, their abilities, and so forth. Men love to stand looking upon these in the mirror of their own minds, as fair faces love to look often and long in the looking glass. This arises from the self-flattery in men that they might always keep their happiness fresh in their eyes. These thoughts, instead of raising the heart up in thankfulness to God, become bellows to pride. They are vain and abominable in the eyes of God. This is seen by how God deals with those mentioned above. For to the one God says, "Thou fool, this night thy

---

1. Goodwin is comparing our thoughts to the sand in an hourglass that quickly runs out.

soul shall be required of thee: then whose shall those things be, which thou hast provided?" (Luke 12:20). To another, "while the word was in the king's mouth," giving him no further warning, God strikes him with madness and brutishness (Dan. 4:31). And Haman, you know, was like a wall that swells before it breaks and falls to ruin and decay (Est. 7:7–10)

Things to Come

This speculative enjoyment of pleasures and sins in the imagination is also seen regarding things to come. Men do this when they set their hopeful thoughts and entertain their desires through vain promises and expectations of pleasures which will possibly be enjoyed in the future. For example, consider those in Isaiah who raise their hearts in merriment as they drink, promising their hearts, "To morrow shall be as this day, and much more abundant" (Isa. 56:12). Or those who say to themselves, "We will go into such a city, and continue there a year, and buy and sell, and get gain" (James 4:13). These forethoughts feed them and keep their hearts in comfort. When they rise in the morning, they begin to think ahead about the carnal pleasures that are coming to them. They think of the advowson[2] or promise of the coming day or week, or of going to be merry with certain people, or going on a

---

2. In English ecclesiastical jurisprudence, *advowson* was the right of presenting a candidate to a vacant church office.

pleasant journey, or taking satisfaction in a certain lust, or hearing certain news, and so forth.

Thus, just as godly men live by faith in God's promises (Isa. 38:15–16; Hab. 2:4), so do carnal men live much upon the promises of their own hearts. They constantly think ahead to what they vainly promise. "Their inward thought is, that their houses shall continue for ever" (Ps. 49:11), and this thought pleases them. And what future pleasures are there, which men greatly count on, that they do not first privately act out in their thoughts? Men thus foolishly take their own words and promises and so fool themselves in the end (Jer. 17:11). They take up the pleasures they are to enjoy beforehand upon trust, like spendthrifts do with their rent or heirs with their inheritance before they come of age to enjoy their lands. Then, when they come indeed to enjoy the pleasures they expected, they prove but dreamers and find their "soul is empty" (Isa. 29:8). Or things fall so far below their expectations or seem so stale as to have nothing in them, so that there was more in their imaginations than in the thing itself. And this arises from the vastness and greed of men's desires. This makes them swallow everything at once—as in Habakkuk 2:5, enlarging his desires as hell, he "heapeth unto him all people," and swallows them up in his thoughts. This is what an ambitious student does with all the advancements that are in his view.

Things Past

This speculative wickedness is similarly exercised toward things past in recalling and reviving in our thoughts the pleasures of past sins, when the mind with fresh delight runs over the ways and circumstances of the same sins, long since committed. Or when men raise up their dead actions, long since buried in the same likeness they were first committed and consult them again—like Saul and the witch did with Satan in Samuel's likeness.[3] While men should draw a line through them and blot them out through faith in Christ's blood, instead they copy and write them over again with satisfaction in their thoughts. For example, the unclean person remembers every circumstance of his immoral acts, and a proud student repeats that important speech in his thoughts, especially the most brilliant parts! So men chew the cud upon any words or commendations about them made by others. Just as a good heart repeats the good things he has heard or read, remembering how his affections were stirred, or as a godly man recalls with comfort a life well lived, like Hezekiah who said, "LORD,… I have walked before thee…with a perfect heart" (Isa. 38:3), and by this stir and provoke their hearts to the same temper again, so wicked men recall the sinful ways of their lives, to draw new sweetness from them.

---

3. See 1 Samuel 28:7–25.

There is nothing that reveals the hardness and wickedness of men's hearts or provokes God more than this.

When someone ordinarily recalls past sins with pleasure, it is an indication that the heart is very wicked. For this is not compatible with grace. For the apostle shows the reasoning a good heart uses about past sins: "What fruit had ye then in those things whereof ye are now ashamed? for the end of those things is death" (Rom. 6:21). For saints reap nothing from all their sins but shame, sorrow, and sadness. When Ephraim remembered his sin, he was ashamed and repented (Jer. 31:19). And can you in your thoughts reap a new harvest and crop of pleasure from your sins again and again?

Nothing is more opposite to the truth and practice of repentance than recalling past sins with pleasure. This again reveals much hardness of heart. For the foundation of repentance is to call to mind our sins with shame and sorrow, to remember them with much more grief than the pleasure we had in committing it. The property of repentance is to hate the very appearance of sin and to inflame our hearts with zeal and vengeance against it. God is therefore greatly provoked, and our hearts are stained with new guilt when we look on our old sins with pleasure. By this, we stand by and endorse our former acts of sin and provoke God to remember it with new abhorrence and so send down new plagues. But if we recall our sins with grief, God will remember them no more (Heb. 8:12). When we delight in our past sins, we are delighting to rub in the wounds we have already given Christ. To view the sins of others with pleasure is in some ways worse than committing them (Rom. 1:32). How much more to view and revive our sins with fresh delight! Therefore, know this, that however much you may here delight to repeat to yourselves your old sins, nothing in hell will harass you more than remembering them. Every circumstance in every sin will be like a dagger in your heart. This was the rich man's task and study in hell: to remember the good things he had received (Luke 16:25) and his sins committed in their abuse. And if godly men are here made, like Job, to possess the sins of their youth (Job 13:26) with horror and, like David, to have them ever before them (Ps. 51:3), how much more will wicked men be continually frightened by their sins in hell? For a great part of their punishment is described for us in Psalm 50:21: "I will reprove thee, and set them in order before thine eyes."

Imaginary Suppositions

The fourth thing in which this vanity of sinful imaginations appears is mere imaginary suppositions. Men pretend and invent in their own thoughts what they would be and do. They create fool's paradises for themselves, then walk up and down in them. What pleasures they would have, if only they had enough money! What honor and reputation, if only they had the opportunity! For an example, take Absalom in 2 Samuel 15:4, who said, "Oh that I were made judge in the land, that every man which hath any suit or cause might come unto me, and I would do" this or that! People dream up such fantasies with pleasure, almost as much pleasure as those who really enjoy them.

This may well be the meaning of Psalm 50:18, where the hypocrite, while outwardly abstaining from gross sins, consents with the thief and partakes with the adulterer—namely, in his heart and imagination, supposing himself to be with them and desiring to do what they do. Take, for example, a man who is naturally ambitious, whom nature, abilities, and education have made to be but a bramble, never to rule over the trees (Judg. 9:14–15), but have instead fixed him in a lower sphere. He is as incapable of rising higher or being greater as the earth is of becoming a star in heaven. And yet, this ambitious man will imagine himself great in his heart. There, in his imagination, he sees himself as great, builds a throne and sits upon it, thinking what he would do if he were a great man or a king.

Or take someone who is unclean but has now grown old and, like a dry tree, cannot act upon his lusts as he formerly did. Yet his thoughts supply what is lacking in strength and opportunity, and he makes his own heart both a brothel and a prostitute. Or take a man that is naturally indulgent and given to luxury: he loves pleasures but lacks the means to buy them. Yet his inclinations will please themselves with various thoughts of the various delights he would have. He will imagine his menu and all that he wishes to have. Or take a vengeful man who lacks a weapon yet pleases himself with thoughts of revenge and thinks up insults and severe criticisms against the one whom he hates yet is not near. As a man in love will court his beloved in his imagination, giving her presents and making solemn speeches, so whatever men's inclinations and dispositions may be, and no matter how great the impossibilities and improbabilities of being or getting what they desire, yet in their thoughts and imaginations, they show what they really are. All that they desire to be they picture to themselves in their thoughts. Men will always be drawing maps of their desires and calculating how to carve out a situation in life that fills their hearts.

And there is no surer way to know a man's natural inclination than by this. For it shows great foolishness, as men imitate children who make clay pies and puppets and pretend to be what they are not—yet such childishness is in men's hearts. This also shows men's vanity because their hearts are set on what is not. The things they desire themselves amount to nothing (Prov. 23:5), but how much worse to please themselves with mere fantasies! Finally, it proves the greatest possible discontentment in the mind when men in their thoughts put themselves into a condition that God never ordained for them.

CHAPTER 6

Practical Uses

Now we turn to the practical uses of this discovery of the vanity of our thoughts.

Humility

Having discovered the vanity of your thoughts and thus your condition, be humbled. I ground this upon Proverbs 30:32, where Agur teaches us to humble ourselves for thoughts as well as actions: "If thou hast done foolishly in lifting up thyself, or if thou hast thought evil, lay thine hand upon thy mouth." Now, just as smiting upon the thigh is an outward indication of Ephraim's shame, sorrow, and repentance in Jeremiah 31:19, so laying the hand upon the mouth indicates a greater and deeper humiliation and conviction of one's guilt — "every mouth may be stopped" (Rom. 3:19). When you are humbled, you have nothing to say and nothing to plead. You do not excuse your thoughts as being free or impossible to get rid of. But, as in Ezekiel 16:63, "thou mayest remember, and be confounded, and never open thy mouth any more," and as in Job 40:4, you lay your hand upon your mouth. This is to humble yourself.

Indeed, there is much cause for humbling yourself. For your thoughts are the firstborn and oldest sons of original sin, and therefore the "strength" of original sin (as Jacob, in Genesis 49:3, called Reuben, his firstborn, his might, and the beginning of his strength). Thoughts are also the parents of all other sins. They are the conspirators, the Ahithophels,[1] who plot all the reasons and rebellions of our hearts and lives. Thoughts are the bellows and incendiaries of all inordinate affections; the panderers to all our lusts that give thought for how to satisfy them; the disturbers in all good duties that interrupt, spoil, and contaminate all our prayers, so that they stink in the nostrils of God.

And if you are not moved by their heinousness, consider their number. For our thoughts are continually at work, making our sins more numerous than the sands. The thoughts of Solomon's heart were as the sand,[2] and so also are ours. Not a minute goes by but as many thoughts pass through our minds as grains of sand in an

---

1. Ahithophel was one of David's cabinet members and a trusted advisor who became a coconspirator with Absalom in his attempt to overthrow David. See 2 Samuel 15–17.

2. This is an allusion to 1 Kings 4:29: "And God gave Solomon wisdom and understanding exceeding much, and largeness of heart, even as the sand that is on the sea shore."

hourglass. So then, even if you suppose your thoughts to be the least and smallest of your sins, yet their multitude makes them more in number and heavier in weight than all other sins. For there is nothing smaller than a grain of sand, but when you heap up sand, nothing is heavier—Job said his grief was "heavier than the sand" (Job 6:3).

And if you suppose that your thoughts are mere farthings[3] in comparison to the defilement of greater sins, yet because their mint never lies still, sleeping or waking, they make up the greatest part of the treasury of wrath which we are laying up. And know this: God will reckon every farthing and will not abate your punishment by one vain thought. To see that God looks upon our thoughts in this way, see the indictment He brings against the old world. It stands upon record in Genesis 6. When He pronounced the heavy judgment of destroying the old world, does He allege their murders, adulteries, and gross defilements as the main cause? No, it was rather their thoughts—which provoked Him more than all their other sins because they were so many and so continually evil (Gen. 6:5).

Therefore, descend into your heart and consider this well. Let it humble you and make you vile in your own eyes. And if one of you finds such treasures of wickedness laid up in just one room of your mind, what

---

3. In English currency in the seventeenth century, a farthing was equal to about a quarter of a penny.

is in all those other "chambers of the belly," as Solomon calls them?[4]

Consider your thoughts that you might be humbled. But for all their multitude, do not be discouraged. For God has more thoughts of mercy than you have of rebellion. Psalm 40:5: "Thy thoughts which are to usward," speaking of thoughts of mercy, "are more than can be numbered." You began but as yesterday to think rebellious thoughts against Him, but His thoughts of mercy have been *from everlasting* and reach *to everlasting*. Therefore, in Isaiah 55:7, having made mention of our thoughts, He says, let the unrighteous man forsake his thoughts, "and he will have mercy upon him." He says this because the multitude of their thoughts might be an objection that discourages them from hopes of receiving mercy. Therefore, He purposefully adds, "he will abundantly pardon." Then, to assure us that He has thoughts of mercy that surpass our thoughts of sin, He adds, "For my thoughts are not your thoughts, neither are your ways my ways, saith the LORD" (v. 8).

Mindfulness

Let us always keep guard over our thoughts. Consider Job's example: "I made a covenant with mine eyes; why then should I think upon a maid?" (Job 31:1). And

---

4. This is a reference to the Septuagint's reading of Proverbs 20:27: "The spirit of man is the candle of the LORD, searching all the inward parts of the belly." *Belly* is a Hebrew euphemism for the soul.

remember this special charge from Solomon: "Keep thy heart with all diligence; for out of it are the issues of life" (Prov. 4:23).

There are other things you are commanded to keep. You are to keep the Lord's Day holy (Ex. 20:8); to keep yourself "unspotted from the world" (James 1:27); to be your "brother's keeper" (Gen. 4:9); to keep all the commandments (1 John 2:3). But above all, you must "keep thy heart" and, in keeping your heart, your thoughts. For this is the great commandment because it extends itself as the foundation of all other commands. For just as the command against murder also forbids malicious thoughts, the same is true of the rest of the commandments. In keeping the thoughts, you virtually keep all the commandments. For just as original sin is said to be forbidden in all the commandments, so the obedience of our thoughts is implied in them all.

Keep your heart and your thoughts, for "out of it are the issues of life." Thoughts and affections are the fountain; words and actions are the stream. As go our thoughts, so go our affections, for thoughts are their bellows. The same is true in our prayers, for thoughts are in the soul as spirits are in the body, running, moving, and acting in all.

God proclaims Himself the sole Lord of our thoughts, for one of His greatest attributes is that He knows and judges the thoughts of men. Kings may attempt to rule your tongues, bind your hands, or control your actions. But only God knows your thoughts. It is supremely in our thoughts that we sanctify Him in our hearts and walk with Him. And shall we not keep guard over them?

And if you look to the work and power of grace, what is it but the power to bring every thought into obedience (2 Cor. 10:5)? This is the glory of our religion above all other religions in the world. For the difficulty and strictness of our religion is in the observing and keeping of our thoughts within bounds. This is what makes it so hard a task. And here lies the difference between sincere Christians and others. True Christians seek to keep their thoughts, for without this, all religion is nothing but "bodily exercise" (1 Tim. 4:8). Roman Catholics may mumble their prayers and hypocrites may talk, but godliness is found in keeping the thoughts.

We are to take care of our words, for Christ said that we shall answer for every idle word (Matt. 12:36). And shall we not for the same reason take care of our thoughts, which are the words of the mind? The only difference is that thoughts lack the audible form the tongue gives them for others to hear. But you must answer for your thoughts as well as your words (1 Cor. 4:5; Heb. 4:12). And if you are careful about the companions you keep—those who lodge in your houses and share your rooms—then how much more should you be careful of your thoughts which lodge in your hearts, which is not your house but God's, built for Himself and for Christ and His Word to dwell in? For you have the most intimate fellowship and conversation with the things that you think. That is why when you think of the Word, it is said to talk with you (Prov. 6:22). And if you are careful about what you eat because of how it affects your health, how much more should you be careful of what you think? For as Tully says, thoughts are food for the soul.[5] As Jeremiah said, speaking of meditation on God's Word, "Thy words were found, and I did eat them" (Jer. 15:16).

Consider the outcome of things. What shall be the subject of that great trial on the day of judgment? The thoughts and "counsels of the hearts" (1 Cor. 4:5). And after the day of judgment, men's thoughts shall prove their greatest executioners. Your accusing thoughts are the whips God will lash you with for all eternity, as you study over every sin, each of which will be a dagger to your conscience. For the torment of the hypocrites will be their meditation of terrors (Isa. 33:18)—to study God's wrath, the blessedness of the saints, and their own sins and misery.

---

5. Tully is derived from the middle name of Marcus Tullius Cicero (ca. 106–43 BC), the Roman statesman and philosopher. Cicero said, "For the study and observation of nature affords a sort of natural pasturage for the spirit and intellect." Cicero, *On the Nature of the Gods. Academics*, trans. H. Rackham, Loeb Classical Library, no. 268. (Cambridge, Mass: Harvard University Press, 1933), 633.

CHAPTER 7

Remedies against Vain Thoughts

Finally, we will consider the remedies against vain thoughts.

Store Up Heavenly Truth

The first remedy is to get the heart furnished and enriched with a good stock of sanctified and heavenly knowledge in spiritual and heavenly truths. For "a good man," says Christ, has a "good treasure of the heart" (Matt. 12:35)—that is, he has all graces and many precious truths. These thoughts are like gold in the ore, which are beat out and coined in words: "A good man out of the good treasure of his heart bringeth forth good things" (Matt. 12:35).

Therefore, if there are not mines of precious truths hidden in the heart, it is no wonder that our thoughts coin nothing but the dross of superficial, vain thoughts, since the better materials which should feed the mind are lacking. This is why Solomon says that wicked men "deviseth mischief" (Prov. 6:14); or, as Junius[1] reads it, they mint or hammer wickedness. Or consider men who have a store of natural knowledge yet lack spiritual useful knowledge. When they are in company with others, they may bring forth good things in speeches; but when they are alone, their thoughts do not run to good things.

For this, consider Deuteronomy 6:6–7, which shows that laying up the word in the heart, being well-acquainted with it, and getting knowledge of it are effectual means for keeping our thoughts well exercised when we are alone. For the reason why we are commanded to lay up the words of the law in our hearts is both to teach them to others and to fill our thoughts when we are in solitude and can do nothing but exercise the mind in thinking.

For when you are walking, riding, lying down, or rising up (for these are usually our most solitary times for thinking, and many people do these things alone), this is the time when you are to talk of the Word. But a person who is alone cannot do this unless the talking meant here is not only outward conversation with others (though this is included) but also talking to yourself. For if you have no companions with whom to speak the truth, then speak it to yourself. For thoughts are the utterance of the mind.[2]

---

1. Franciscus Junius (1545–1602), who studied under John Calvin in Geneva, was a significant figure in the development of Reformed theology in the late sixteenth century.

2. This is a reference to the teaching of the Hellenestic Jewish

This is evidence if you compare Deuteronomy 6:6–7 with Proverbs 6:22, which suitably interprets it. For Solomon, exhorting to the same duty of binding the word to the heart, uses this motive: "That when thou awakest, it shall talk with thee." That is, by thinking of the Word, it will talk with you when you are alone with it, and so you will not need a better companion, for it will always be speaking to you. This is the fruit of binding the Word to the heart.

Preserve Spiritual Affections

Second, endeavor to preserve and keep up lively, holy, and spiritual affections in your heart. Do not suffer them to cool off. Fall not from your first love; do not lose your fear or joy in God. Or, if you have grown careless, strive to recover these affections again. For your thoughts will follow your affections, which incline the mind to think of the objects which please them, rather than others. Therefore, says David, "O how love I thy law! it is my meditation all the day" (Ps. 119:97). It was his love for God's law that made him think about it so frequently. So also in Malachi 3:16: "Then they that feared the LORD… thought upon his name." Fear and thoughts are joined,

---

philosopher Philo of Alexandria (ca. 20 BC–ca. 50 AD), who distinguished between the spoken word and the inward word. See, for example, Philo, *On Abraham. On Joseph. On Moses*, trans. F. H. Colson, Loeb Classical Library, no. 289 (Cambridge, Mass: Harvard University Press, 1935), 510–11.

for what we fear we often think about—and often speak of as well, for it also says, "and spake often to one another." Fear made them think much of His name; and thinking of it made them speak of it. Indeed, thoughts and affections are the mutual causes of each other: "My heart was hot within me, while I was musing the fire burned" (Ps. 39:3). Thoughts are the bellows that kindle and inflame the affections. And if the affections are inflamed, they cause the thoughts to boil. Therefore, newly converted men, having strong new affections, can think with more pleasure on God than others.

Consider God's Character

Above all other impressions, get your heart possessed with deep, strong, and powerful impressions of God's holiness, majesty, omnipresence, and omniscience. What thoughts of power can more settle, fix, and draw in man's mind but thoughts of God? Why is it that saints and angels in heaven never have a vain thought for all eternity—not even one wayward stroke. It is because they are fixed by God's presence; their eye is never off him. If you take a loose, brash, unrestrained person and put him in the presence of a superior whom he fears and respects, he pulls himself together. Job guarded his thoughts so as not look astray because he lived in God's sight (Job 31:1–2). This is also what drew in and fixed David's thoughts. See Psalm 139:1–12, where David shows how he was continually grasped with thoughts of God's greatness, majesty, and omnipresence. What effect did this have? "When I awake, I am still with thee" (v. 18). When someone wakes up, the first things he thinks of are those objects which leave the deepest, strongest impression on his mind. David's thoughts of God left such a strong impression that when he awakened, God was first in his thoughts. Therefore, we find by experience that one means for avoiding distraction in prayer is to expand our thoughts to God's attributes and His relationship to us. Do this in preparation for prayer or when you first begin to pray, and it will make you serious.

Start the Day Well

And when you wake up, pay special attention to your heart, as David: "When I awake, I am still with thee" (Ps. 139:18). People eat a good breakfast in the morning to prevent the fatigue that comes from an empty stomach. In like manner, to prevent vain thoughts arising from an empty mind, fill your heart in the morning with thoughts of God. But know this: when you first open your eyes each morning, there will be many thoughts vying for your attention, like so many clients or suitors at the door. But speak with God first, and He will say something to your heart to settle it for the day. Do this before business crowds upon you. It was said of some heathens that they worship as God whatever they first see in the morning—and so it is with the idols of men's hearts.

Keep Watch throughout the Day

Have a watchful eye and observe your heart throughout the day. Though thoughts crowd in, notice and observe them. Let them know that they do not come into your mind unseen. If a man would rightly pray, he must watch who comes in and goes out. Where a city is watched with vigilance and the police are observant and careful to examine all suspicious vagrants, there will be fewer people in the streets. And if you do not keep a strict watch over your heart, it will be filled with swarms of vagrant thoughts, making their rendezvous in your mind.

Guard Your Eyes

Do not please your imagination too much with vain and curious sights, but guard your imagination by guarding your eyes. This is why Job said that he "made a covenant" with his eyes, lest he should think on a maid (Job 31:1). As Proverbs 4:25 says, "Let thine eyes look right on, and let thine eyelids look straight before thee."

Focus on Your Work

Be diligent in your calling, and "whatsoever thy hand findeth to do, do it with thy might" (Eccl. 9:10) by putting all the intention and strength of your mind into it. Let the stream of all your thoughts run to turn your mill.[3]

---

3. This is a reference to a watermill that would be built on a stream or river, so that the water would turn the turbine, providing power to the mill.

Keeping your thoughts to that channel keeps them from overflowing into vanity and folly. Those that do not work are idle, wandering busybodies (1 Tim. 5:13; 2 Thess. 3:11). They are not only idle (because not busy with their own work) but also meddlesome busybodies (because they meddle in things that do not concern them), going from house to house. Similarly, when we neglect our work, our minds wander, having no center.

When David walked alone on his rooftop, what sinful excess his spirit ran into! If you let the ground lie fallow, what weeds will soon grow! God has appointed our callings to occupy our thoughts and give them work. This keeps them busy in the intervals between the appointed duties of worship. For the spirits and thoughts of men are restless and will occupy themselves with one thing or another.

Therefore, as kings keep men with strong, active spirits in constant work, lest their minds should be working and plotting something sinister, so even in Paradise, God gave the active spirit of man a calling to keep him busy. By this God hedges in man's thoughts and sets them in a narrow way. He knows that if they are unconfined and given too much freedom, they will be like wild donkeys sniffing in the wind (Jer. 2:24).

But take heed of burdening the mind with too much business—with more than you can handle. This made Martha forget the "one thing...needful," for she was "cumbered about much serving" (Luke 10:42, 40, respectively).

This breeds cares which distract the mind, and divide it, and so cause wandering thoughts. This weakens and enervates the mind. And this brings vanity. As Jethro said to Moses, when burdened with business: "Thou wilt surely wear away" (Ex. 18:18). You will be like a fading leaf with its moisture dried up. The sap which should be left for good duties will be exhausted. As dreams come through a multitude of business (Eccl. 5:3), so a multitude of thoughts comes from being overburdened with business.

Commit Yourself to the Lord

Finally, in your calling, and in all your ways, commit your ways to the Lord. Proverbs 16:3 says, "Commit thy works unto the LORD, and thy thoughts shall be established," or ordered—that is, kept from confusion, disorder, and the swarms of cares that annoy others. By this, your aims will be accomplished.

A few thoughts of faith would save us from many cares and fears in our daily business. This shows how vain our thoughts are, for they do not even help us move forward with our intentions. So, when such waves toss your heart and bring turmoil within, when the winds of passions are strong, bring a few thoughts of faith into the heart and all will soon be calmed.

How Thoughts Reveal Our Hearts

"Where your treasure is, there will your heart be also" (Matt. 6:21). These are the words of Christ, our judge who discerns the thoughts and intents of the heart (Heb. 4:12).

No man's heart is in his own keeping. But whatever his treasure is, that his heart will love. If God is to be made a man's treasure, He calls for the heart: "My son, give me thine heart" (Prov. 23:26). But if any earthly thing become man's treasure, it takes away his heart: "Whoredom and wine and new wine take away the heart" (Hos. 4:11); his heart goes after covetousness (Ezek. 33:31).

Consider Your Treasure

Your chief and dearest thoughts are spent on your treasure. Therefore, go down into your heart and examine yourself. What consumes your thoughts and attention? What are the eyes of your mind fixed upon? What brings you delight and is never far from your mind? That is your treasure, and it has your heart.

Someone who is passionately in love delights to remember in his captivated imagination the likeness of his beloved. He pictures her in his mind, for thoughts are the only way of bringing someone absent into the heart. Similarly, the soul feeds and increases love for whatever it desires by thinking about it. Affections chain the thoughts and fasten the mind and attention to the object of love.

As an example, just think of a person's outward treasures. Those who have precious jewels love to look at them. They love to open their bags of treasure to count everything inside. So it is with the mind. Time and again, the heart views and visits its object of love—its treasure—with thoughts. This brings it fresh delight and a sense of security. If, for example, the soul treasures its "goods laid up for many years" (Luke 12:19), thinking of wealth brings a sense of ease to the mind. On the other hand, men who love reputation love to think over their past accomplishments. Others, taking pleasure in some future sin (such as uncleanness), anticipate its pleasure in their imagination, rolling it over in their minds again and again, like actors rehearsing their lines.

This is something we all find: that the greatest pleasures of our lives occupy our thoughts, so that when we are unable to enjoy the things we desire, we delight in imagining them. This entertains the soul, until it enjoys them.

We can see in the Scriptures that men are distinguished by the objects of their thoughts and the musings of their hearts.

Also the schemes of the schemer are evil;
He devises wicked plans....
But a generous man devises generous things,
And by generosity he shall stand.
   (Isa. 32:7–8 NKJV)

You can be certain that what men spend their
thoughts devising indicates what they are. If they "mind
earthly things," then they are earthly men, "whose end is
destruction" (Phil. 3:19). And one of the things that dis-
tinguishes the godly from the wicked is that he meditates
on God's law "day and night" (Ps. 1:2). David's purpose
in this psalm is to differentiate between different kinds
of people. And there is a good reason why they can be
distinguished by their thoughts, for one is known by his
companions—a man's disposition is known by his friend
who knows him best. And whatever a man thinks about
most, this he makes his most familiar friend. We best
know and are best known by our thoughts, for through
our thoughts we take things into our very hearts. That is
why Solomon in Proverbs 6:22, speaking of meditating
on the law when one awakes in the morning, compares it
to conversation with a close friend: "When thou awakest,
it shall talk with thee." And this is why a man is called a
"friend of the world" (James 4:4; see also vv. 1–3).

Consider Your Character
Men's thoughts reveal the distinctive character of their
hearts. This is true because thoughts are the freest acts of

the mind. In thoughts the mind is most itself: "For as he thinketh in his heart, so is he" (Prov. 23:7). Therefore, as the saying goes, "thoughts are free."[1] And in this sense, it is true that of all acts, thoughts are the least enforced and follow the free disposition of the heart. Men cannot speak or do whatever they want to, for their words and actions are subject to enforcement. Therefore, one can be deceived in judging men by their speeches and actions. But a man can think whatever he wants. And, indeed, men usually pore over whatever pleases them. In their thoughts they act most like themselves—regardless of their outward acts. We do not know the true character of stage actors as they play their roles on stage, but if you see them in their dressing room, there they act like themselves in their base, lewd dispositions. In like manner, the thoughts are the dressing room of the soul, its most private chamber.

As the most direct acts of the soul, thoughts show its quality. For thoughts are the fresh-minted coins of the heart, bearing a replica of the soul's likeness. To get the true taste of a grape, savor its juice when it is freshly squeezed in the winepress before combined with other mixtures.

Not only this, but thoughts are the most continuous acts of the soul. The soul abounds in thoughts more

---

1. Possibly a preference to Paracelsus (ca. 1492–1541), a Swiss physician and philosopher of the German Renaissance, who said, "Thoughts are free and subject to no rule. On them rests the freedom of man."

than anything else and, therefore, are most revealing of the heart. Of all the faculties of the soul, the thinking faculty is always working. It is like a little wheel in a jack, moving twenty times faster than anything else. Even when we do not have the liberty to satisfy our desires, our thoughts are working. The heart cannot be kept from thinking about what it wants to enjoy. Christ calls the thoughts the treasure of both a good man and a bad man, because thoughts are abundant in both: "For out of the abundance of the heart the mouth speaketh. A good man out of the good treasure of the heart bringeth forth good things: and an evil man out of the evil treasure bringeth forth evil things" (Matt. 12:34–35). You see, when Christ gives the reason for why men can be known by their words, He compares the heart to a fountain, the source of thoughts and words.

The surest rule of knowing the character of the heart is to study its most abundant thoughts. Every good man has a treasure and spring of good thoughts within, which no wicked man has. And though his good thoughts are sometimes mingled with the mud and filth of vain and sinful thoughts which often obstruct their flow, sooner or later, the spring works itself out again. The current rises and keeps its course—though perhaps through many twists and turns. Just as rivers eventually flow into the sea, so there is a spring in his heart that tends Godward. Another man, though he may have a flash flood of good thoughts, they are soon dried up again, but there is not a deep spring of good within.

Compare two verses from Proverbs 12. In verse 2, the wicked man is called "a man of wicked devices," or imaginations. In other words, he is a man full of wicked thoughts. But in verse 5, we read that "the thoughts of the righteous are right." This means that the current or tendency of his thoughts is toward that which is right. His thoughts are exercised about righteous things.

Consider David in Psalm 139:17–18, who says that the thoughts of God are precious to him, more numerous than the sand. This may be interpreted to mean his thoughts about God, which are so many that he says he cannot tell their total sum. For, he says, "When I awake, I am still with thee" (v. 18). But of the wicked man it is said that "God is not in all his thoughts" (Ps. 10:4). And in Jeremiah 2, God rebukes His people, saying, "Can a maid forget her ornaments, or a bride her attire? yet my people have forgotten me days without number" (v. 32). And in Proverbs 6:14, the wicked man's heart is said to continually forge mischief, like a smith forging and hammering iron. And because his thoughts are vain, the wicked man's heart is said to be worth little (Prov. 10:20).

Answers to Two Objections

Now when good souls examine themselves in this, they often make two objections.

The first objection is that evil, vain, and foolish thoughts frequently swarm upon them, especially when they have solemnly separated themselves to seek God in holy duties or on the Sabbath days. Therefore, they say, "If I should judge myself by my thoughts, the world and a thousand vanities must be my treasure."

But a man should not judge himself merely by the multitude and noise of these thoughts. For these swarming, buzzing, humming thoughts arise naturally out of the heart, as Christ says. And the imagination of man's heart is evil continually (Gen. 6:5). And even for most Christians, it is certain that the bulk or quantity of the unregenerate part is more and greater than the regenerate part. The regenerate part is greater in power and carries the heart against corruptions and has strength to steer the course of a man's life, especially in great turning points. And in the end, Christ will bring the regenerate part forth to victory. But in spite of this, if a man measures his thoughts by the bushel, he is sure to find much chaff mixed in with the good grain. Instead of counting thoughts by their quantity, you must make your assessment by the hospitality you give to vain and worldly thoughts once they have risen in your heart. Do you indulge and nourish them through delight, so that they take root in your heart? As Jeremiah says, "How long shall thy vain thoughts lodge within thee?" (Jer. 4:14). How long shall they lodge, nest, and find the most pleasant welcome and harbor? Do vain thoughts settle comfortably in your heart as your best friends and most pleasant companions? Do they lie down with you and talk with you when you awake, with deep pleasure and delight? God's words in Jeremiah can be likened to a father asking his son about riotous friends and lewd company: "How long shall your vain companions lodge in your house, eating you out of house and home, to the neglect of your wife and children?" So it is here: "How long shall thy vain thoughts lodge within thee?" How long shall they prey upon the best part of your heart and your dearest affections?

The regenerate in respect to vain thoughts is like a man who walks through a dust storm or swarmed about with little flies in summer. He shuts his eyes and holds his breath but cannot keep them from coming, even though he tries to swat them away. But to the unregenerate, these vain thoughts are like the air he gladly breathes. They are his element.

A man's thoughts about his treasure are most pleasant, delighted thoughts. They are not dry thoughts; they are drenched and deeply soaked in the affections. Such thoughts embrace and entwine the affections, such that the affections say, "Wherever you go, we will go as well. We will welcome whoever you bring with you." But when vain thoughts swarm into his heart, the godly man refuses to let them lodge there. He goes often to God for a whip to send them away. These thoughts may trouble you the most when you come to holy duties, for your unregenerate part wants to disturb and hinder you. It is strange that before prayer, you may try to remember something but cannot. Then, as soon as you go to your knees, such thoughts come instantly! The devil also waits for just the right time to interject thoughts. To be sure, just when your heart is coming to those things in prayer that you most need and long for, that is when you will be struck with some distracting thought that, before you know it, you will instantly be hurried away. In this regard, I sometimes say that a man must learn to keep a negative Sabbath—that is, he must attend to the negative part of holy duties. His task in such is to set a guard and lock the doors against the troops of vain thoughts that come crowding into his mind. Or, if they do come in, to keep kicking them out again.

Like our father Abraham, who had to drive the birds away from the sacrifices (Gen. 15:11), so it is with us. Abraham could not keep the birds from coming down again and again; but he could drive them away when they distracted him from the primary duties of devotion. And so it is here: while the best of souls cannot keep the unclean, ravenous birds of vain thoughts from coming down upon the sacrifices of their devotions, they can strive to drive them away.

The other thing I would say in answer to this objection is that although vain thoughts may be far more in number, yet when you look at the whole course of his life, the heart of the regenerate man still follows God, returns to him, and keeps on its way. He is like a spaniel that follows his master on a journey and runs after every bird and every flock of sheep he sees. The spaniel may expend more energy and run over ten or twenty times more ground compared to the way his master goes. Yet for all this, he is still sure to have an eye to his master, returns to him again, and follows him to the journey's end.

The second objection concerns our worldly affairs. Are not the thoughts of godly men to be taken up with their worldly business? Are they not to think through and plan out what they should do, especially when it concerns their calling, so that they spend most of their thoughts on this? And if so, how can we use our thoughts as criteria for assessing our spiritual condition?

A good man must diligently do the work to which he has been called: "Whatsoever thy hand findeth to do, do it with thy might" (Eccl. 9:10). Yet, the heart must also be poised and carried throughout the day by the habitual fear of God. "Be thou in the fear of the LORD all the day long" (Prov. 23:17). These two commands from the same pen do not contradict one another. When a servant attends to his daily business in the presence of his master, he can be both intent upon and sufficiently thoughtful of his work, while doing so with respect to his master. And there is a habitual reverence which both awes and poises the mind so as to do nothing which is unbecoming before God's presence.

Next, observe your thoughts when your work is done. What do you think about when your heart is free, in your spare time, in the morning, or when you lie awake at night? What are the tendencies and haunts of your heart at such times? Observe this the way you would observe a servant, who though he works diligently when kept at home, yet uses his free time to frequent some other house. Similarly, watch the haunts of your heart when you are free from your daily work, when you are free in your thoughts to enjoy whatever you want. There you will see the secret treasures your thoughts seek to unlock and view with delight. The wicked "deviseth mischief upon his bed" (Ps. 36:4). He does not sleep until he has wallowed in the imaginations that naturally suit his spirit, for these lighten his heart and make way for sleep. But the church says, "With my soul have I desired thee in the night" (Isa. 26:9). And David remembered the sweet songs in the night he had together with God: "When I awake, I am still with thee" (Ps. 139:18). And consider Proverbs 6:22: "When thou awakest," the law of God, like a companion, "shall talk with thee."

Finally, if you are overwhelmed with thoughts that keep you from the free air to breathe up to God, you will find your heart like a mole underground, heaving and digging upward, tossing up the earth that keeps you under, till you are above ground.